The Humorous Side of Aging

Bringing Heart Warming Memories With Aging Laughter

Judy Deutchman

Ebook formatting by
www.ebooklaunch.com

You might also enjoy

Prayers For The Children
Of The Single Mother

Author Judy Deutchman

Available on Smashwords

I want to personally thank all my
readers
For sharing the inspiration
And memories we will cherish
always.

This book is dedicate to my
children who are grown now and
my husband whom I love growing
old with.

Contents

Chapter 1
Grandmas Job Search Log

Observing my fogged up mirror after a morning shower, I jumped with shock, dropping my towel the minute I felt my husband's hand grip my ripe old butt. He described to me that he was just trying to grab an apple from the basket. I told him that was a nice compliment because other than my body, apples are taut and firm. He then said that it was more like a soft well ripened fuzzy peach. How nice it is to still feel desirable at this age. My husband with a silly personality reminding me of my favorite cartoon characters, is good to me.' With a giggle I could not hold in, I continued with my morning routine, leaving the towel on the floor at this point. Using a dry towel with one hand to clear away the steam and holding firmly onto my coffee cup with the other, I centered my attention on counting silver threads piling over my auburn color that I proudly covered a month ago, while pondering if it's all worth it. I'm truly out of work for the first time at fifty five. Three months have gone by, taking with it a small nest egg I never thought I would have to depend on, at my age.

I remember not long ago, in my youth, before the family life, still getting a full time work schedule and holding down two jobs. I was able to party all night, while sleeping at work on my lunch break. Thinking back, it seemed so easy. I am not calling myself old yet, for the proof of the generation of eighty to ninety call me part of the young crowd. I for one hope that's not what I will be like, telling the middle aged they are young people too. If I do, please let there still be the existence of hair dye, allowing myself to feel I have a memory that gives me a wish of being young at heart. I do recall when gray hair never mattered. It was all about grandma and grandpa coming for a visit, letting their hair turn gray and figures pop in all directions. The grandkids ran for hugs and kisses, while secretly wiping off their kissed cheeks. Getting our little cheeks pinched, wishing and hoping it didn't happen again, trying to avoid it at the end of the visit. I would give anything for that now, without the fidgety feeling of running to hide so I could go behind closed doors to wipe it off. Time has passed and grandparents are no longer one hundred percent there, being replaced by daycares as the parents go off to work. Now, in our middle aged lives, we are looking for work, losing the memory of the big garden in the backyard full of the tallest corn stalks. Sweet potatoes and carrots hiding under the ground with a tip of green decor and most of all, Mr. Scarecrow standing watch.

Being a nurse for close to thirty eight years, I grip on not going down in silence. We are the In-crowd baby boomers; fluffy, plump and full of hugging and spoiling our outstanding grandchildren. As our time draws near, we can only hope to see in-home caregivers driving us where we want to go. We will be dreaming of having clean homes, with our meals prepared, while joyfully sharing our stories of the old days. Sounds like a pretty good dream after all the years of picking up after our children and husbands. Fantastic payoff to finally be able tell others that work for us to do the dishes and laundry, give us a bath and cook a nice hot meal. Becoming involved with the State as an Independent Healthcare Provider, the last five years, was a breath of fresh air. Having a single unique patient to care for individually in their own homes had been less taxing. Spending a majority of thirty years working in hospitals, nursing homes, then retirement inns including home health care, age suddenly puts into perspective what I'm unable to do anymore. Indeed, I am in the middle, so still young, not old at all, with the realistic situation at hand. This has made it tougher to find work. What's the matter with me or is it that the younger generation is ignoring my knowledge? Now I am facing the age bracket of watching the young get the job first. I want to be standing in line ready to work, putting my age behind me with an unending balance of faith. I looked forward to meeting each interview with a client that clearly ends up being as timeworn as me or a few years on me. Heading out for possible employment as I go from different meeting places for interviews working in the direction of regaining my health insurance or should I say life insurance, which both has been on pause for four months due to reduction in my work hours. I thought financial depression was over in the eighteen to nineteen hundreds. I personally lean on faith for all I go through and more so at my age now. Things take place for a reason, so I must trust in knowing that these are life lessons to a higher blessing.

Job interviews in the fifty year old and up age range make us become motivated because we are the people of expertise. In any case, it's not taken casually by ourselves as professionals now. My first job call comes in, so I'm now a human being of the working senior group, plus someone wants me. Somebody that wonders more about the number of gray hairs I have than my years of skills. When getting ready for a job interview I try not to think of the flash of time, back when I applied for my first nursing position landing the job freshly out of school.

Dressed and organized for this, I recognized what to expect as I was ready to go for it. A few months earlier, I found myself working with a client close to two and a half months. This was before my asthma kicked in so bad I had to excuse myself from that position with a doctor's note due to my health problems and the environment of the work situation at the time, the client was a hoarder with four cats. She lived in an apartment with cat urine including filled litter boxes that were never cleaned.

In addition to the health concerns I was having, I stayed, thinking it was just a cold I had, when in fact my asthma was not agreeing with me being the right person for the job. With uncontrolled coughing and shortness of breath, causing dizziness, I thought I was over doing it with sex at my age.

Three to four weeks later, I got my breathing back under control, but at the same time I was still looking for work. The days turned into weeks, then months. As time flew by, I saw myself still out of work. I was writing more than ever, enjoying myself so much more than I could remember.

My daughter lived with me and my husband. We were supporting her due to a disability she has had since birth. She was my only client. With a few hours from the State I was able to cover our rent. Outside of that, all the rest was taken care of by my husband.

This was telling me that it's time to have someone take care of me. I have followed the will of faith, after all the years of holding it all together with my children as a single parent before I married again, now I was being taken care of by my family, while I continued writing and publishing my books.

My next job interview was coming up with a call I personally received and I was determined to get my thoughts together. I was going to grab this job, no problem, I may be older, but I got this. I was confident as I headed to meet my client and for sure new job. Coming up to the front steps I knocked on the door and a very nice young lady opened the door asking who I was. I specified being there for an interview and she replied that she did not remember anybody coming for that. I was asked to come in to meet with the lady who forgot about it, leading me to tell her about myself as I proceeded toward the client. We talked a little while, maybe a half hour or so, before she asked me to follow her downstairs to where the clients were, not one client, but three residents/clients living in her basement apartment. In just a short time it all went downhill. The lady showing me around, younger than me of course, startled me by unexpectedly stumbled over one of her client's wheelchair leg rests and down she went, head first on the cement floor. My maternal instincts took over and I proceeded to take all measures to do the right thing in making sure she was alright. She looked up then she tried to stand. At that moment I noticed her forehead was bleeding and knew the interview was never going to get anywhere. I can still see the ambulance coming to the front door as I found my way back outside telling them I just came for an interview. Let me give myself a few minutes of pause before I go into another job conversation experience. Of course I have to get the mood back again. In another way I meant to say I need to get the middle aged faith fight back, plus must go onward. If there is a bus ride to age fifty and plus I do not remember formally accepting it. Yet, if in fact I did, then I just don't have any recollection of that moment in my life. Supposing there is a lot of rules and regulations to go with complete snags to get out of that one. Things were somehow stress-free when we were younger with the option of needing a job or just to save for a first car or because you were dating. One more day meant another dollar spent on an interview at one o'clock. How unusual to see a caregiver, who seems to come across as a family member, waiting for my arrival. The family was apparently looking for more care hours. The next lady I saw was the daughter not the client who was not there, but supposed to be giving the interview. She set herself aside right away, letting the caregiver in training start asking me questions. Seemingly the client did not know how to give an interview, which is fine in some cases if the client was there. Turning out to be a rather odd afternoon as the questions kept coming from the caregiver that apparently only just met the family and was hired a month ago. It was an awkward meeting but I got through it as they were hoping that the daughter could understand the interview process from a far-fetched just hired caregiver who has not been known long and it still in training. I just got there so hire me or at least let me interview myself. This was not for me as I professionally got up and spoke of another obligation I could have had. It made me feel like I was at a children's daycare learning center with no teachers. On my continued interviews I was simply becoming affected by unpleasant encounters and totally supposing the worst by now. Deciding to take a deep breath and carry on with confidence.

Let's see how this goes as I drive downtown to another possible paycheck. Arriving at the front door a young woman was watching me as this was inside a senior community home apartments. I saw that she may be a caregiver. The young woman asked if I was coming for an interview as her client was talking about it earlier that morning with someone on the phone before my arrival. I said yes of course I am and asked how she was. She appeared hurt in that moment. She mentioned she was out of town and just returning to work when her client notified her she was going to be getting another caregiver to take her place, clearly misunderstanding that she did not quit her job, but just went on vacation. She started to get tears in her eyes and confided in me that she did not want to lose her job. I was going on another interview from another planet. I may be at a ripened middle age, but I am an experienced counselor by now. She waited outside while I went in to get this over with as soon as possible. It became the most emotional situation of tears, sadness and gloom. Next thing I know all concerned are in the room and I am not ready for the involvement of this one. Wanting to walk out at this point, I continued to hear both sides of the story, encouraging both caregiver and client so I could get them to come to an understanding. The young woman wanted her job back and I had to get going. Either way something had to give. With another problem solved or job saved then I'm a hero again. Going to another interview and why not, God is using me and I know this because this time I was sent there to heal the hearts of the troubled and confused. Each time I touch a life in trouble God heals it through me and how marvelous is that?

Back in the ring, another interview brings a lot of negative drive I don't want to feel right now. I must keep my faith so my bad energy will not show within my presence, in any professional surroundings looking for work. In time I continued on searching for work trying to care when I don't seem to anymore. I am most likely just tired and its way past nap time for me. This next interview was to be held on the fourth floor of the Library downtown at two o' clock. I went up the elevator fifteen minutes early, finding a chair to sit in and wait for my familiar newest client to come through the doors. I remember the description she gave me on the phone. It was two thirty and I got a phone call from her daughter explaining that her mother was running late. A half hour late with my past interviews in mind I sat waiting and trusting this was to be the job I will get. Finally, coming out of the elevator door a young woman walks right by me. I did not recognize her nor her me. A few minutes later I see an older woman coming out and we both said hello. I just realized the first young woman was her daughter. She introduced herself and me to her then we found a place to sit. The librarian said we were too loud for a meeting and asked us to take a room across the hall that had a closed door. More privacy I suppose as we had a wonderful visit and all seemed well with the contract signed. My start date was in the next few days. We said our goodbyes then a couple of days went by when I called to see what time I was to start with this new client. She responded that she did not know, plus had no paperwork from the case manager yet. So I waited another few days to call again, getting the same response and that she just did not comprehend the contract. I called the case manager and she mentioned to me not to wait on this client because she had not got a hold of her either. Keeping this in mind, that closed within a few weeks. When I stepped back and looked in on this situation, there was an understanding that warmed my heart in a way that I never could have imagined. The Mother was to be the client, but her daughter that has disabilities was caring for her Mother until they hired care.

Seems I've been sitting on the couch most of every day looking for jobs online. I get sluggish and flabbier or maybe just freshly plump is a much more delicate way of putting it. With each day that passes, I don't seem to be the same person with the equal motivation as I did when I was younger. The following week's drag on for me and I find myself wanting to do less and don't want to try as hard as the day before. Of course I do have to contact at least three jobs a week to keep my unemployment coming and I know I could just call any three on Monday morning asking if they're hiring then write them in my job log sheet taking the rest of the week off. I am actually trying to find a job I might truly want to do. I'll admit that I might be subconsciously avoiding finding work. My age is a problem for some employers, I know. I can tell when a potential employer sees me this way, looking at how many gray hairs I have. They show a sort of surprised look on their faces. I have been around people too long not to read the expressions of those situations, all the while I stay, hoping I'm asked about my experience, not my grays.

Chapter 2
It Can't Be Easy

I decided taking a break from it all. Taking off to the lake to go fishing. I went floating out on the rubber raft. I set sail with my husband more than just fishing in mind. In a short period I became so involved in the sport I wanted to go every day. One of our fishing trips was a lesson learned. There is a limit to how many you can catch, which is five. We had strung them on the boat from the chain hooks and after catching our last of the five, we went to string it, only to find that the chain was gone. As a fish story goes, make sure your husband ties the chain tighter. The most unmemorable at fifty five is when I wish my memory was short lived as I had to go pee real bad and I am out in a lake on a rubber raft holding it in. My husband can go the easy man way while telling me to do the same by hanging over the rubber raft waist deep and just let the warm sensation of urine run in my pants in cold water. My bladder hurt bad as I tried to do so when I slid to hold on to a log in the water trying to relieve myself. Not happening in cold water, after unsuccessful attempts over twenty minutes time I realize that one has to have warm water to pee and I am hanging there with nothing happening, wondering how you men do it. I decided I needed a real toilet, so swimming off to shore I went, so I could walk one half mile around the trail to the campsite bathroom, dripping from head to toe of course. I can tell you one thing, it is a good workout with heavy, wet clothes, running to pee that far. Of course it was a relief to finally let go, as I had forgot about the walk back and not so eagerly the swim. Walking back to the water, I was wishing I had let loose in there because it was a swishy washy feeling being drenched. Either way, I was wet but felt much better. We stayed later that afternoon because we had our limit by eleven am before we lost the chain of fish and of course had to start over. That afternoon we caught four more fish. The views are breathtaking while fishing on the boat or by land, watching the fog lift from the lake and turn to sunshine on the tips of the water. The time passes by so quickly and before we knew it, it was time to head back home, leaving peace behind until we go again and somehow never want to leave. I thought about how it felt to have such free time. I did not want but in time could not do without. Thank you God for the beauty of the earth and giving me peace for a time.

It's been near forty years of working, raising my children, counting on a monthly fixed income from employment to survive each day. It is now a different world as it seems I have been waiting for this moment of retirement to come. Now it seems retirement has come sooner than expected. I've become more comfortable than troubled with my salary, which brings me closer to writing my thoughts down into soon to be published books. My life has changed so fast over the years of course. No more insurance and no work made for further inspiration to write more. Finding other talents I am good at is rewarding and fun, including swinging at the park, if you don't mind the looks. Passing time with new ideas made me realize over fifty is not a rusty age. I felt like a kid again, learning wonderful new tasks my brain can take in. Enjoying life for the first time, I have to say I for one am completely forgetting about hard times, work searches and unpleasant stories I can only thank God for.

While at the lake, one day, we had a couple around the age of sixty to seventy. We were all sitting together and talking for over three hours. This for sure was an inspiration from God. Somehow the wife of the couple became so interested in my discussion about how I love to write and involving a book I just published. There I go again having a talent I am good at that someone else found of much interest. Yes a great feeling to see in others that talents at my age can be so remarkable. She had even said I should go on book tours and be on camera telling my stories.

There should be a lube and oil for after fifty to keep us believing and loosen us up so we continue to stay motivated, holding our chins up. I gave a break to interviewing and focused on my writing full speed, for a while, as more education with publishing my books, I have learned, has become important for the present time. Pleasing long walks were loved as we passed horse farms near our place along the way plus within a short time we made friends with farmers and horses. Learning about horse treats instead of carrots seemed to be important to the owners. We were buying carrots by the bag a couple times a week costing us more money than healthy treats made with real oats, which was better for the horses. Cheaper on us to get a big twenty pound bag of apple oat treats and it would last us at least five months. We are called the farm walkers now and the owners want us to let them know how the horses are doing and if we see anything unusual. That is a wonderful pastime, giving us exercise while loving the horses and making friends. God wants us to love and take time to see the beauty of the world when we go on in tough times to give us strength.

I have had part time work in between this, but nothing compares to my writing. I have found photography is a wonderfully enjoyable reward with the places we go: fishing, mountains, lakes, rivers. I will remember my life now with pure satisfaction as somehow my talents have become great interests. On the other hand, suddenly, I am getting the feeling after a few long months, that something is absent. With my husband getting laid off, things became less gratifying. It's not surprising for me lacking work but still wondering why I have to tolerate my spouse when we used to enjoy the company of each other while one of us was still out of the house on occasion still working. We have done a lot together since he has been home and now we need to find time away from each other. Pressure builds and the decision to want the house empty for time alone of course adds to the stress of who is going to go where first. I said goodbye to my husband as he very much needed to get out and take a long drive for the day so he is not staring at the walls. Doing everything together, I had to come to a wakeup call that the fifty plus retirement and or out of work meant go away I just want to love you again. I thought it was rough when our kids were teenagers and now I feel this way about my spouse, trying not to believe it in fact happens at our age. Its lunch time already looking at the clock tells me fifteen minutes after twelve as times flies when you want to be alone for a bit and I feel like I just had breakfast. Now having lunch soon gives me the great opportunity to check the mail. How exciting, as most retired seniors look forward to that. Starting to lose my confidence in the work field with the months of time going by, I find it hurts emotionally, more each day. I do believe it's a nurturing feeling of wanting to be needed. I continue to get calls for work, but sad to say most of them I can't do anymore. Like lifting and heavy duty full care patients. My bone degenerative disease is part of my middle age life now. I am sounding less assured as how good I still can be is turning into I can't. This focus however must push me toward God's plan and faith while I continue writing again, so if all else fails, write with God.

I suddenly saw a big difference in my husband. The more upbeat I became, the more he became down. It brought him to the deepest of lows in depression. Not finding work and blaming his faults on me put him in a situation I did not want to see, like looking in a mirror with me out of work too. It was awful as usual when he gets this way so I kept going on and I did. He fell behind me because he felt lesser of a man. At his age, it's not too certain because we all have more than less when you think about it. More plump with added skin creases gives character. I was coming to a realization that letting go is a good thing while letting God take over. This was the hardest thing I have ever done. I saw my husband go from the man of my dreams to someone I did not know. I for one had to get separated from him so I could stay strong only because he would not accept he had a problem. I could not help him, only someone of a professional background could. I did say need of professional help in this case I still believe middle age has qualifications to help each other. I don't plan on charging my husband for putting me through years of emotional crisis nor him me. He was staying with a nearby neighbor due to traveling being harder at our age for a short separation to keep our sanity. I am now at two weeks of waiting for a return from him to give me good news that he has decided to accept help. I am giving the tough love, which is the most impossible thing to do to the heart after so many years with this man. As my heart breaks, it is like a death of a great time off with him all summer with good memories. I only pray in time he does the right thing just to come home. In the meantime, I am going forward for whatever reason, I have no choice, keep writing while I go through a tender time in my relationship during the golden years hurts as much now as it would a high school love.

It's been a few months now and my husband and I have had

some very long talks and getting
more of an understanding of who
we are as a team old or not. We
were married a team years ago
with young love and trust. I look
at the man I married coming to
some real life realizations about
each other. Finding out that it is
not just about him, but me too.
We understand that we have
issues to work on and no one
person is to blame. My husband
has been supportive of me at all
times and me him. I learned that
yours truly still had control issues
from back in the eighties when I
was a single mom. I can do it all
was the feeling I always carried.
Getting too close to anyone who
would take that away from me
was a distress. I have struggled
with that for years till my husband
came along. I can say I really did
fall for him, watching from the
ground as he was up on a ladder
at his work one day. Not seeing
where I was going I slipped and
fell on my butt, twisting my ankle,
along with breaking my leg. He
took care of me, so love
blossomed. If he works with me I

can work with him without fear
and rejection. One of my hardest
trials in life with relationships I
have that failed because of it. We
all have setbacks in life due to
our own insecurities. This takes
me back to thinking we knew it all
at a certain age in our lives as
teenagers. Not a true statement
at all. When you see yourself
going through emotional drama
you feel there is a certain age in
maturity you reach where this is
supposed to stop. No such luck,
as we are always learning and
thriving, no matter how young or
old. I believe it is not a sense of
age to come to, but a maturity to
handle it with a stronger attitude
and using our heads and hearts
to make it in our golden years.
Every day is a new day for us as
we continue to look into the future
of living more presently than to
keep bringing up the past pain
and old school thoughts. We
must go on for us and never go
back to if, when or what. Which is
harder to say because staying
back in time can be an escape
from old issues of years ago. We

have refined with age, turning those feelings to positive thoughts as we age, thriving through a new life without regret. When we catch ourselves letting go, trusting God because we have to so he can mold us into the reason we are here every day. Through all trials of life no matter what they are we choose growth not fear in the years to come as we age.

Chapter 3
Hire Me I'm Worth It

A few more months have gone by and I received a call for an interview. I had been busy building my videos for my blog concerning my book with no interest now of going. I had to keep preparing to go forward as my life was changing every day. I got ready, then showed up right on time and I saw another caregiver there. Certainly not the one that was leaving a job opening for me. As I walked in the apartment all I heard was gossip and rude remarks from the client and the caregiver about the one that's leaving, which is nowhere in sight. She positively should have her ears burning by now! Embarrassed, I sat and listened for forty minutes about the horrid stories on this poor girl who was not there to defend herself. Maturity is underrated, in this case becoming the same age as my clients wondering if my gossip has gotten that good by now. Not a surprise to even be on the same medications, besides how scary is that? I then quickly excused myself and mentioned I had another interview and was on my way to the door when the client asked me to call her if I do not get hired with anyone by the end of the week. She would then want to hear from me. Hey, I got years on her, so might I remind her close to the same age. I thought, if you want me hire me now, don't wait till I see someone new. I never felt so close to feeling sixteen again. Who do they think they are? I left and got into my car with relief, playing one of my favorite tunes on my radio called, "You are so complicated". I however quickly changed it to a Christian music station with praise songs, to realize I must pray for these people.

The weather was getting windy and cold so my husband went on fishing trips without me. Continuing to write, I was surprised one more call came in for a job. Off to the interview convinced this sounded good and I had positive feeling. I called the client back and we chatted for a while as she told me I was her last hope and no other caregiver could give her flexible hours, but I could and will. I showed up for the appointment with gladness as this time I was determined to get my insurance back up and running after becoming sick with bronchitis as it also affected my asthma in a bad way. A few hundred dollars later I was out of the doctor whom I saw outside of my regular health care community and left the pharmacy of my choice and two hundred and fifty dollars later not happy seeing a strange doctor who did not know me. You can understand my regular doctor would not see me paying cash or not. My personal coverage had not been renewed yet. Without it, I could not be seen at all by the health community I belonged to. I do know how embarrassing it is to spend cash money out of my own pocket for full medical care at my age. Being uncomfortable about whether I am thought of as strange for having no coverage or look rich for not needing any just throwing my empty pockets around to pay for such needs. I wish I could have felt the security of being comfortable with my needs being met through aging then the unforeseen future of job hunting. During the interview I saw the client had five cats and I thought this is fine, because it was a clean home with well managed cleanliness. I was told by the client she wanted someone who had a personality like, "Whatever". I was asked to show up by just dropping by anytime, no set date. I came by at ten am, appearing to be reasonably professional as we sat and visited for over an hour without getting to the clients daily living plan of schedule. Instead, she agreed I was the caregiver for her and said she would call the case manager. Four or five days goes by, so I call to see what's up. Come to find out the client did not remember my last name so she could not give it to the case manager. On to calling the case manager and tell her my name as she knew me but in this case a loss of communication for sure. It is another waiting game on a signed contract, for a few more days. I waited three to four days and saw nothing. I do feel at this point my writing is most contenting. Waiting still for more answers to some kind of a future for me through God as it seems where I have been and am going.

Sunday night and I am looking forward to Monday so I can get some more information if I am getting a new client or not. Positive thinking is wanting to have my sunny weather back to go fishing and walking to the beat of retirement, the way it was before the rain came. I will admit there is no problem with me not having a passion for healthcare anymore. But more the ambition to follow God's will on my next assignment.

Tuesday afternoon brings exhaustion from a long night of

no sleep with my husband as we were stressing over the fact that we have not been getting along. Together twenty four seven, starting to get to each other, as we almost called it off with our relationship. My faith had to get to my heart as I prayed for peace that night and morning. When it is just what's all around us it can feel like we are not going to stay together. With God's will and faith we strongly regained the hope back. Realizing it brought peace and understanding to a better level, holding on with our wrinkles and set in my ways, staying in love.

Then a call came in on a job for me with the one I had been waiting for. I start my new client in the next few days. I myself am thrilled with a smile and ready to get going and receiving my insurance back. Starting, my new client was fun and exciting with her upbeat personality. Our days were filled with laughter and her five cats. Trying to get my hours in as much as possible to fifty five for the month got me as far as twenty two hours because we were working every day. I was determined with only a week and a half left in the month of thirty days. The client called me one morning. I was to go past twenty two hours and she said a cold was coming on continuing to let me know her throat was sore too. She asked me not to come in that day. I was waiting for the phone call to see if she would be getting better. I hope all is well as I am still praying this client will stick around. My unsure insecurity at my age was more than relieved to hear from my newest client three days later, after I called a few times. Getting no answers I was enlightened to learn she was looking forward to seeing me come in to work the following morning. The trust I am gaining back with my faith will get me on the straight path. I need to keep positive. After all, up till now I have had several awkward moments of unsatisfactory unemployment with complete confusion. Someone of my age group just could not give up or write a book that will help others fifty plus to keep booming to survive. I am doing great as my newest client is so upbeat and supporting. Who said work is not fun and rewarding? This gives me time to write with the hours of the new client. Being so happy and on the right road again was a blessing from God.

I continue to remind my heart daily not to get so involved in things so deep, but just pump that's it. It took only near a week with this new client to go from happy to be working again to a heart filled with more than I could take because by the end of the day I was emotionally in tears. My client had been struggling most of her life, remembering years ago with her children too. She wanted to share a meal with me at a share house for the homeless near-by. I walked in not feeling uncomfortable, but like I did not belong in a room full of homeless, hungry families of all ages with small children living on the streets. I felt empty at the same time with some kind of regret. The longer I stayed the more my heart just wanted to help these people in need. How could I help in times of such a circumstance where everywhere I turned I felt helpless? We have given our whole lives and now fixing anything, if possible, comes so close to the soul. Getting in line for a free plate of hot food brought many hugs and smiles from one another just to keep going forward. My turn to get my name on the list with the first question they asked, "Are you homeless?" In my view, looking around the room seeing people with families who had no place to live I then quietly said no. Turning to stone I could not move as I asked how I could help donate here. I was told by the surprise on the young man's face volunteering that he would give me a card at the end of the meal to give me information about donations. My deepest thought was I do not need to be here to eat their food. I wanted to go so bad, but something came over me. With the support my client needed, I did my job, but somehow wanted to do more as I ate my hot plate of food that I felt did not belong to me. I learned from that experience God must be showing me something. I am still learning for now. I do know that if you are of this middle age life it's not always figured out, no matter what your circumstances are. All I could take with me after work that day was how I felt in a crowded room of homeless families. I prayed to God why did he show me this, then a strong sense of spiritual warmth came about me as my heart took me back to the long years of wondering when I could feed my own children, raising them on my own, before meeting my dear husband after my first book about being a single Mother. Writing about focusing on single parenthood and the dream to help those single families, even if its twenty years later, would have never been too late. Being in the share house reminding myself what happened to me and my three children years ago after the fact is still happening to more families every day. My story was lived already, with many more families still hoping for a better reality.

Our children were the focus of our lives when raising families in our earlier years. There was always an appointment to be somewhere. High school plays, football, dances, cheer leading practice, homework, dentist appointments, doctor and the list goes on. We were busy with our children, every day wishing for a moment's peace to drink a cup of coffee or tea that was not cold after sitting several minutes mostly found in the microwave or forgotten about hours later. Now our children are adults, with families of their own, hustling through life as we did. This time we are wishing for that phone call just to say hello or let's have lunch, which never seems to happen as often as we want. There is another generation out

there we are a part of by
watching it grow before our eyes.
No more can we scold or control
our children in the way it was
when they were small and so
dependent on us. Sometimes it
can be weeks or months before a
holiday or birthday comes up
when we are the ones who call to
make plans for a get together. Of
course, everyone shows up for
what took a few weeks to
prepare, only to see it go by like a
second hand on a clock. Just like
it did when the children we raised
were little in just a flash, grown
up, out the door, going back to
their own homes. You are left
only wishing you could have that
heart to heart talk again about the
first love and broken-hearted blue
eyes looking up at you for
support. How does the heart of
wishing we as the once busy
parents get past that feeling, to
be secure with what we created
so proudly? The answer is
memories in our minds to ease
the hurt of not a loss, but another
growing period of maturity in our
middle years. I remember hitting

the snooze button in the morning for work when I was younger, lying in bed as long as possible, contemplating calling in sick because I wanted to sleep. Now, I say I have to get up before the alarm so my body aches will subside within an hour and my medications are taken on time. I miss the days when I could just get up and go. No pain, no pills, no nothing. Just do it by getting the kids up, fed breakfast, dressed and ready for school, while you cram in time for getting yourself ready. By no means did you forget the morning coffee that's cold already. The good thing about working now is I can enjoy that cup of coffee. Then again, calling it the truth, I need it more now than back in the days of raising my kids. Being back to work it's wonderful to see that paycheck again every month.

Chapter 4
I'm Still kicking

Above all, I have encountered
some health problems again, but
this time it was due to a weight
gain from May of 2012 when my
father was diagnosed with brain
cancer. I got really concerned
and loved him so much as I
remembered how well he was
just a short time ago it seemed. I
gained nearly 15 pounds I so
desperately tried to get off a few
years ago with my husband,
walking every day with the horses
and eating healthy. That dropped
fast when my father became ill.
Now, four months after his
passing, I began to go through
the process again. I just got back
in the swing of things after
stopping my regular routine of
exercise, walking, and eating
healthy. Now I find my asthma is
becoming a problem again, with a
diagnosis to a stronger inhaler,
which will take a few weeks to get
used to and feeling better. Then I
am told my thyroid is a bit low

and my cholesterol is a little high. Back to better eating and fish oil gel tablets, which is good for what ails me when it comes to lowering the fat in my diet. I took out enough already so I see a stress factor here causing all this because of my father's passing. Here I go in my wonderful fifties in what I hear are the best years of your life.

Six a.m. and I am at the hospital with my client, who is having surgery on her nose to help with breathing problems. It was a long day as check in was seven a.m. and I was thinking this would be only half the day. It was one p.m. before I was told she was still in surgery, possibly getting out to go to recovery in an hour. I waited till two thirty when I could finally see her. Making phone calls to get her family to come get her and take her home by seven p.m. because I had to go at three thirty. Arrangements were made so I could be relieved of my work for the day.

Not less than a week later, my client got a call from the police waiting to hear where her grandson was as he was on the streets and getting into the wrong crowd many times made her worry so much. Her grandson was shot and killed at three a.m. and devastation set in. I gave her a few days to stay close to family members coming in town for support.

The big snow storm came in on Thursday instead of the actual day it was supposed to come, the following Saturday. It snowed for three days, including two snow storms and twelve inches of white fluff. Everyone was house bound for a week and so glad to get out when it was safe. I was ready to return to work, while my client is always concerned about my safety. I waited one more day as she was still having nightmares and emotional moments concerning the loss of her grandson. I stayed strong for her, trying not to think of just losing my father a few months before, holding it together. In our time, when remembering being young children, we see our grandmas, grandpas, aunts and uncles pass on. Now, in the golden years, it wakes us up and hurts deeper than ever before, seeing life just go by too fast.

Having four days off from work because of the snow was nice with having so much time to take drives to the falls. Nearby, about ten to fifteen miles apart, with two beautiful waterfalls just waiting for my camera to take pictures of white cliffs with mountains that followed high up above landscapes. Splashing waves rolling down onto the bumps under the water, different shapes of rocks hiding from the sound of thunder the falls made as they hit most of the earth like an instrument of song. It took all of the stress from the emotional days with my client the last two weeks away for the moment.

Returning to work was full speed ahead to help my client get everything the family needed, such as balloons and markers-to write loving memories on them, for a last goodbye at the site her beloved grandson was killed. It was a good day to send off balloons. Watching them float up into the sky, I got the strength from God to stay professional and strong through it all, for my client because she needed me. Had I done this in my younger years of twenty to forty you would see me in tears. Now, I find myself, by the grace of God, carrying such a profound respect, knowing it's not about what I am doing. In fact, I have learned through my life to really be there for people.

Doing my best to keep the faith, I found myself becoming more involved than I realized with this client, through the loss of her grandson. As we get older, the maternal instincts to care becomes stronger. It hit home for me more, with the loss of my father not too long ago to cancer. After work, I continued to take the sad story home with me and soon felt the professional side of me stay at work, then at home I had to let the stress out. Not a good idea when your family tells you what you are acting like. It was a double whammy holding in my feelings at work and coming back to a peaceful house to have my outlet.

Getting so close as a caregiver makes you feel like family, so if they hurt we hurt. In this particular situation, I am glad I handled it in a sensitive way that worked for both of us with my husband taking the credit for his support in the idea. I may think I have it all figured out at almost fifty five now, but I find that no matter how old I am, learning lessons are unavoidable.

Working with my client on a more professional than personal level was really working out. I felt less stressed and more in control of my surroundings. My family is happier, of course and with my husband finally back to work at a Temp agency full time, things are finally looking up. With my husband back to work, it gave me more time to write my books and more time to myself, which brought our relationship to a healthier level. We have never been happier. We only have my daughter at home, so yes my husband makes dinner a number one priority. Now, this may seem a terrible thought, but sometimes when I am writing I wish more time would exist.

My husband is not perfect, he is human. He has kept me from harm's way, plus he is the man I came to love dearly for many years. As time went on, I also saw more love from him. I kept reminding my heart and mind to start new behaviors and let God take over, so that's what I did. I let God take over completely. It wasn't about me and what I thought anymore, but it was about what God could do because my Father was passed on now. I had no one to blame but myself for not letting God in, all the way. From when my father divorced my mother I held that

pain in and it was time to let it go.
When you're halfway to one
hundred time speeds up.

Chapter 5
Middle Age Growing Pains

Going fishing the other day
seemed to go by slower than
usual for some reason. Why did I
not enjoy it as much? I had my
daughter on my mind, including
the problems she has been
having with her back the last year
and pain management. From
shots, to MRI's, to X-rays and
more. Many thoughts were racing
on in my heart and I was praying
it will all be ok. Remembering she
is my angel born of special needs
at birth and no matter what, she
is still my baby at thirty three.
Being a mother who loves her
children young or old, this is the
birth of an aging wild cat if my
kids are in pain. I could put it with
such a lighter note "Do not step
over this line!" To this day, my
daughter still has back pain, even
after her shot a month ago. She
will be seeing the doctor who
gave her that shot in the next
week, then she will see the
neurosurgeon to confirm whether

or not surgery will take place. I am not getting too old to love my kids. No matter what, even if I am one hundred, I will still be there, carrying all levels of compassion.

For my daughter this is the day that has come too soon-a final answer on whether or not she will require back surgery. We entered the doctor's office and waited as the doctor was fifteen minutes behind, which turned out to be almost two hours. It was bad circumstances because my daughter was so tired of being in back pain for so long in the last few weeks that she fell asleep on the examining room table. The doctor arrived, rushing in the door as if this room was the finishing line to a marathon. My daughter then fell into tears as it's been overwhelming for her for some time and it just had to come out. My emotions were going haywire and I became near tears. When my baby hurts my heart comes out of my chest. The doctor examined her, coming to a conclusion that surgery was no longer an option but a must.

Her appointment was for two thirty, but the waiting again took us to five p.m. talking with the doctor, he explains not what he said a month ago which was if the back shot does not work then she should have surgery. It came as a shock that he's against surgery and decides that stronger pain management is in order. I am so glad I am much more mature as my temper wants to fly higher than this doctor's thoughts. A second opinion is what comes to mind after all this. I am not happy as I pout inside myself angrily and leaving confused. I was not looking forward to square one, seeing my daughter's physician first thing Monday morning, to find a different neurosurgeon. I could have stayed and had it out with the doctor, but my daughter was crying and very confused.

Monday morning is here with my daughter's physician about her constant back pain. He had some common sense to say that there is no need to cause stress over all this and that we can't force the neurosurgeon to do surgery. Alright, so staying out of the ring of fire through all this I am supposed to not feel stressed anymore? Sure that's simple as long as I take my happy pill. The one that helps with staying calm, or the one making me forget it all. Why does age have different factors? To stress or not to stress? I just want to be retired and what they call "Living the life". We are now headed for aqua therapy for my daughter's back problems as we are told it will be a lifetime problem and will need to maintain this for pain management. Is this the aging process? I have lived this and now to see my daughter go through it in her thirties. This is a double whammy for me looking for the grease shop for the middle aged. Oil me up so I can keep going, wondering why it's her and not me. I am supposed to have all the pain and troubled body aches, not my daughter, so young. There was another episode later on for my daughter about being diagnosed with TMJ, which is the worst jaw pain ever. The first few weeks she was prescribed high doses of pain medicine and physical therapy for her jaw. Continuing on doing this for three weeks brought us back to going to the doctor again for an evaluation. My daughter's pain became so unbearable the doctor suggested a much higher dose, mentioning that it will go away. He also said to put her meals through a blender with no chewing, but to just swallow, so as not to use the jaw. We carried on with this method for several weeks before coming to a conclusion to go see the dentist, who felt x-rays were not necessary, telling us it's just TMJ. Less than two weeks later, I'm taking my daughter into the ER, finally getting x-rays done. In conclusion, the exam at the hospital showed she had a molar, which is a tooth deep in the back of her mouth, near the jaw pain, that was infected. So back to the dentist to have a molar pulled. The only good thing is, I can relate to her so much more than she will ever know.

Another day at work with my client and I am finding myself wanting to just leave and go home. Knowing my daughter is near if anything else goes wrong I'm where I want to be is what I need. Sitting at my computer with endless thoughts of words coming from my soul to my fingertips still memorizing each letter for all words turning them to paragraphs and pages for my desire.

My writing passion that beckons me each day becomes stronger. This is the unique aging years calling me again as I sought after for a moments time grasping those dreams I can never replace. I though I felt stronger in my younger years within the longings I now am carrying inside become much more meaningful today. Fifty and plus years are growing so much faster I almost hate the thought of being that young child I once was. Behind the school desk thinking of nothing but waiting for the bell to ring. Class is over and soon the years will pass, eagerly waiting till I am eighteen and free. Was I free then or am I free now at fifty five. That's the question I may answer with some regret or disappointment. The honest truth, I can admit, I was free then to learn all the world had to offer and now, years later, taking what I once took for granted am able to put the pieces together where they go. Maybe all the parts of life, up until now, are just borrowed parts of the full world to piece together and I can start making sense of it now.

Youth and retirement calling me again in between the moments of my heart. I take a deep breath connecting both worlds for a minute or two, maybe longer waiting for thoughts I would not normally have. Lessons learned I can recall seeing the two ages collide. Thinking about what I can remember when I was young, naive and quick thinking about the white picket fence; being married with two children a boy and a girl, followed by happily ever after. God gives us birth with the excitement of life and love, ambition to run and play. We have nothing of knowledge for what we are in for with living life as we believe we'll never age, being like a child always. Then growth happens with broken hearts, learning the hard way to lean on God and grow our faith. With that said, we can now tell stories to our younger generation, watching them give us looks like nothing like that could ever happen to them. So why are we not to ever know the secret of aging when we're young? The birth of youth, but not that of the birth of age will be a mystery to the wee small ones that are God's children. We are all God's children, no confusion here, as the teen years turn to adult years, then growing old slowly begins to show us the birth of age. My eyes look into my reflection that compares me to a mirror image of my childhood days. That's all I see for a short time I feel the smallest world I want to get lost in. That of the child I once was, to be able to fall in when our thoughts carry us back so as we age they can stay alive and never fade. It has to be what keeps us going is the youth no matter how the silver threads grow in numbers in our hair. We hold on to chasing our rainbow. I know my youth is gone in my face as the mirror speaks the truth the child seems to stay.

We are the greatest artist to our grandchildren.

We definitely have had experience with that for a fact. I still love to create art as I did when I was a child. I believe art can be a talent we cherish as age continues on. The aging process, when it comes to puberty happens again as the forties go by and suddenly you're over fifty. Then you have age over sixty and seventy telling you you're just a baby to them and they say "Just wait till you're my age". I personally have found much of a struggle in letting it happen to get older with what I call another generation of age transformation. Thinking I can handle this as smart and mature as I have been, I suddenly became scared that my body is what it is and will no longer fit into that size again. I shall never mention as you may have found out by now. This is pain in my heart or should I say my thighs? I thought this had already surpassed me in my transformation from teenage to adult with a surprisingly significant decrease in childhood moving towards acceptance of aging without fear. Trying to hold on, stressfully taking on emotions of trying not to let go when it is so much easier for God to take it all. I prayed for this with my answer from God helping me along these next few life changing stories as I continue to write. Speaking of the teenage and younger years settling my mind back in my forties when clubbing and dancing was still available for me. Moving like that now would possibly break something or leave me in a permanent position calling it a new dance move. I see my client's daughter of fortyish finding a man in his thirties looking for a room to rent. My client has an apartment for lease, so he moves in as her daughter continues to have a relationship with this young man. Being of my age, I do not agree with such immaturity as to have a man or young boy move in with me while my daughter dates him. May I say they only met two weeks ago and were hitting the sheets so fast. The walls are thin, keeping my client up nights. I am not there of course only in the daytime hearing these stories of the mother, which is a client of mine. Seeing them call each other pet names I have no judgment over this due to the fact I was wild back in my day. So now why do I find it horribly disgusting? My opinion only, don't get me wrong, of course, there are days now that I am gladly not going through the new puberty of adult to middle aged again. How funny it is that I keep telling myself it did not at all feel wrong when I was doing it at that age and not the same situation at all. How is it that we feel now it's just not right, but then it was? Does seeing this behavior remind me of such memories? I am going to continue with this client because it's a paycheck. I am not too old that I meddle in others business, that will happen when I am elderly, right? I have not matured to that age yet, but I am at good practice with the older than me clients. Well after thirty eight years in nursing care I got to start somewhere, so now is the time to learn all about the next aging process. Here I am bringing up the forties. As you know, my husband is forty-five and I am soon to be the ripe old age of fifty-five and a young ripe I might say, so far. With this in mind, I do feel like I am seventy or eighty because it can emotionally at times drag me down, making it hard just knowing I do have energy and can still walk my three mile walks, which I did today, finding it so enjoyable. I am learning a good lesson here, to never let yourself go to the extreme of not being able to keep up with your spouse because it can make you feel sick in many ways. My bones ached more, which made my headaches worse, with energy levels going down instead of up. Only ten years apart, that's all, so I really have to stop making myself get old around him when I am still in my prime. Of course my thoughts and being set in my ways could put that together. I then went on my usual three mile walk again today, which I had let slide for a few months. I did it with no problems. I am not too old that I forget my fifty-five years of education whether it be from hands on experience or a good book of life's challenges. I then can say kindheartedly that you are as young as you feel. Stop counting my faults, I keep telling my nerves more often than not, but still I wonder if they are terribly worse now or better?

I'm finding myself wishing I could change some things that happened earlier in the day, as I try to sleep one evening. Several contemplations dancing in my head, wishing I could solve all thoughts come morning. I am mature and older, so I have to handle these thoughts better.

Faith is the answer to stopping me from focusing on the negative. Returning from a day on the river with our two new little one man rubber boats with oars, enjoying my family, but finding out still I don't have the hang of this boat oaring yet.

Chapter 6
Blast From The Past

Determined to set out on my own, I am finding myself going in circles again as last month with my husband fishing. But this time I went full steam ahead, clear out to the middle of the lake, rowing and rowing side to side and in circles, until I had tears in my eyes, which my husband could not understand. He, of course, rowed up to me to comfort my frustration. Here we are me with tears running down my face and my husband asked, 'What happened to you?" I tried to tell him through tears of heart ache that I was not the boat champion. I could not stop crying and absolutely had no idea why I was still in tears. Boats held together by our hands holding each other, just floating. Proceeding on the water I got a grip of life right on the lake. Wanting so bad to master this sport in seconds, I could only think of how much easier these wonderful adventures were still in my heart and mind, but physically, absolutely could not do anymore. I got angry for a moment and it felt so good. I was sure I could beat the rowing down. Aging is a process for me first hand and all I wanted was to be young again, letting the anger go and accept what I cannot do anymore. I am not unsettled at all about venturing out with determination because I learned that no matter how hard it is to accept aging, I rowed back with accomplishment. With little trouble, my husband so kindly stayed close by, both boats tied together with a rope, floating in the other rubber boat, making sure I got back with a smile and I did. Finding the lack of control over the rubber boat to my struggles in life I may never manage to get rowing down. I will be working on not trying so hard to always be stronger than I already am. Let's recall memories when we were still able to function one hundred percent, dancing to our kind of music. So come on, if we hear our music full blast, from the past we would jump, right? Quick to judge of what kids listen to now. Younger generations jump up to their music so in return we jump at them. A perfect example, I remember one day my siblings and I were up on a Saturday morning talking loud and listing to our favorite music. To our surprise, we got yelled at by our parents, as they wanted to sleep in. Not happy with us at all, they gave a lecture on early morning noise being a bad idea. Thinking nothing of it, we went about the day, being normal teenagers, driving our parents crazy. What a surprise when the next Saturday approached and at a much earlier time than last Saturday my siblings and I were woke up to the loudest music of the sixties my parents listened to! Us kids jumped out of bed and ran out to the hallway, not even awake yet. My parents were very happy with their little joke. I believe we got the message with a hands on reality check. Nothing physical at all, just mental awareness that

Lawrence Welk is not the teenage dream! Indoor movie theaters have it lucky now a days with warm heaters and comfy chairs. I can recall outside drive-in movies, holding on to a speaker, your car window only able to close half way with a big chill coming in. Hoping with anticipation the wires attached are giving you the satisfaction of not sounding like a radio station going static. While trying to fine tune, turning the tiny knobs on the speaker box then gladly turning on the radio in the car to tune in the station the movie was on. The lines for food were horrid, as we had to leave a movie there is no pause button to head out for another box of popcorn. I sometimes hardly had a care as a teenager with a drive-in date you're not watching the movie anyhow as we forget the five friends in the trunk who we brought in free. In our day, a scoop of vanilla ice cream was all you got. Taking two seconds to plop it on a dish. Nowadays, it takes twenty minutes to decide what crazy flavor you want. Simple food items have gone from one flavor into many choices now. A nickel for a hamburger in the fifties was a simple item on the menu. The movies were fifteen cents for Disney films, including being able to see two movies for that price. I recall going to the shoe repair shop to see a cobbler that could fix your shoes if the soles were worn down. Dropping them off for a week then picking up brand new souls to wear. Now if your shoes are old, we give them to goodwill or throw them away. Shopping downtown was fun with many shops open to browse through for holidays before there were any malls. All stores were separate and in different parts of town, while now if you went downtown, it would be considered unsafe.

There was the time a friend of mine was riding in my car off to the mall, she at forty-five decides to turn one of my old music DISC'S up to roaring loud. I might listen to it on the highway full blast, but stop at a light and turn it down so as not to let everyone hear or see my younger age music outburst! She leaves it on full blast and made it the most embarrassing moment of my life. How bad I wanted that turned way down at the stop, but my friend was rocking out to every beat, loud and clear, while I hide myself in my hands turning red as the Corvette next to us comes to a stop. Let's look back to our younger years when that was cool. It is now the time of my maturity with my mother when it takes a break and cracks for a time or two meaning more than a crack bringing a large leak to surface. I just have to remind my mother not to fight with me. I do get into it with mom when we don't see each other for a few months, then her demands on me, telling yours truly I need to spend more time with her. It gets harder to be there twenty four seven for my mom when I am in the middle of my prime and close to fifty-five, working full-time with family grown and building a life for my daughter's future with disability challenges. In fact, I do see my mother, so there's no guilt trip here, is there? Let's make this clear and simple because my mother and I have our girl time as she calls it. My mother decided to move again, at seventy-seven years old, into an apartment from a retirement inn she lived in for fifteen years. Getting so busy with looking for a place and moving, I would say the last three months have been hard on her. I do feel the same way about my kids, but I don't demand their time as I would love to or be legal to anymore. My mother targets me with emails. I am surprised to see her announcements of my distance from her like its illegal or something. Why do these things come up as I age? Can I be scolded by my mother at over fifty? I agree my mother honesty tries to make me feel like I am a child again. I thought I got this age thing down, but I do believe I am on my way to another age acceptance by maturity. I found myself getting mad inside and just emailing back to say my thoughts. I did just that and my mother responded by saying we will have to just agree to disagree, leaving it at that. Thinking that I was lost and suppose she is getting tired with frustration of all the moving, staying with a nearby friend, which in fact is closer than me. I did offer for her to say with me, but she refused due to other plans. My mother, however, is a busy lady, with energy ready to burst at any given moment. I did assure her that things will settle in when she is all moved into her new place. How many of us get upset when we do give the world to our parents as they age, yet we are still called young and they say wait till you get to be my age? With the way things are going so far, I don't want to be their age! I suppose being called very young at fifty-five is just senior experience by means of critics being branches in the way that you just shove a side on a nature walk to aging.

Fighting does not get any easier at any age. When hearing my husband's stress after work and he just blurts out something rude to make my whole day fall apart. I go completely silent towards him the rest of the evening, with tiny little growls and looks only a new couple in their twenties may endure. This lasted a couple hours after I made a great meal for him, after my long day and that rude remark because of tension from my husband took me to not caring about my age, but wanting to run to the ocean for a few days, weeks, maybe months. I am old enough to let this go, so moving on with my life should happen gracefully, instead I used silence and growls. How funny is that now? So immature on my part, my goodness how old do you have to be when it all stops? I believe it now when I hear, no matter how old you get you'll never lose the child in you, so pout all you want middle aged baby boomers. I still love the swing if I could only fit in one. With this all said, I can go on writing about my life experiences, putting aside the idea I will ever have a full total gym-fit body. When indeed my families full energetic needs is my own personal total gym, all in one. With emotional and physical uses not that of my tone body by the way, but that of my sanity.

Chapter 7
That Old Nurturing Feeling

Since I'm talking about exercise,
my client is sixty-six years old,
getting many interruptions of her
own type of family fitness
involving cats. Every time you sit,
you're up again, going after one
cat or another. As a caregiver,
I've walked into many homes in
my time, but this one, well it's a
dose of five cats that are indoor
and some extra outside strays
she feeds on occasion. That will
keep you busy. I should say, it
definitely makes a house a home,
when the nest is empty of
children, off and grown, replaced
with a favorite pet or in this case
pets. Very healthy and well
maintained with an individual
name for each one. Bringing out
the personalities for all. Being of
middle aged, I can and still have
a memory to remember these
cats' names. Here it goes, Hans,
who is gray and close to eight
years old and seems to think the
walker my client has is his to ride

on as she pushes him around the house daily. Then there is Oreo, who is black and white, looking like a cookie. He will lay on the floor until you stretch out your arm to rub his belly as long as you can, which he will never want to end. Levies is an orange and white cat who seems to be annoyed, will hit you with a soft swat to your arm if you do not notice him all the time. Midnight, who is black, of course, has some moves you only see when petting his back in just the right spot. He will then shake his head back and forth like he is rocking to music. Tanoak is a long haired loner, but loves to be loved for short times as he is the only one with fur that sheds to fly all over the house within minutes after sweeping. Never forget to mention Pixie Ann, a Siamese, as she is so lovable you hold her for half an hour put her down then she pops back up on your lap for more. Now Penelope is a short-haired outdoor cat that's a stray, but hangs around for food and love, with independence all her own. It may take time to name them all, but that does not include the love you have to give them as you say hello to each one.

It is amazing to see a fulfillment for this client. I have seen her care for these cats that fill a void from when she was younger and raising her children. The instincts are stronger and overprotective, like they are our children. Pets are a big deal to the retired community. Now there's Sable, a long-haired tabby found in an alley at two weeks old, in which my client is the nurturer of all lost cats. This kitten is still in my client's life four months old now and healthy as can be. A stray that's called Mamma kitty stays outside and scared of all people. Pretty well comes around for food and water outside only. Jake is a short haired black kitten who meows as if he's talking to you twenty four seven once he gets started. His family left him behind when they moved. Two more to mention as they are the latest kittens, Tiger and Shadow. Eyes still closed at the time found, at a race car track, in an abandoned race car. They all end up at my clients home as she nurtures them back to health and finds homes for them, well most of them. Interesting as we find ourselves still wanting the satisfaction of being needed after our children are grown. I admit I have a grown adult cat named Sasha that turned four this year, which brought my need to look for another kitten. What is it that tells us our nurturing days are not over no matter how long the kids have been out of the house bringing up their own families? Probably the fact that we are not allowed to control our grandkids. Ouch! That hurt more than I thought it would, still wondering whose mouth that came out of. Just picture this, all at once you have your children back at home with their children and your cats that are supposed to fulfill your empty nest longing. Remember the cats were with you before the kids moved back in. You want your kids gone again, right?

When the children leave the nest it's nice to visit them on occasion so we can hope to have a pet to replace the loss. I can see it now when you explain why there is a pet in the house that was never allowed before. Worst of all, it becomes your baby and never goes outside without a leash so there is some control still in the house. If we can't control our kids and their kids, then we find a pet that don't talk back. Oh dear, tell me I am not seeing my kitten grow to be four month's old already making me lose my baby! I am going to seriously consider a fish in a water bowl and heaven forbid it ever floats to the top. Memory is one subject I have yet to mention if I can remember such events. My clients for me being a home care nurse for the state have problems with memory at the same time I am getting forgetful. They tell me that some days I am not all there, like my mind is somewhere else and it is, but I have no idea at all, until it's mentioned. Then I have to re-think what I am doing, like my mind is really becoming lazy. I do have to take time, letting my mind wonder one of these days, just to see where it's going. I can then tell who ever asked me what am I thinking when I am not all there. I believe we all want to know this. I call it multitasking to a degree, that maybe what I am doing at work is not of interest to me anymore, so I slide by it with ideas of writing in my thoughts. Everyone is different with many places in general you might be at when your mind wanders, too. For middle aged, I honestly feel my mind does wander into the unknown until I write it. There are so many new ideas in our thoughts so as we get older the old goes out to bring in the new with trying to remember the old and where it went. I wish I never knew where it goes at times combining memory with emotion. In reality, we find ourselves getting so impatient, trying to find or remember something that got lost in the space of time. I hate to mention the fact I found myself getting so resentful towards my husband after a long hot day of ninety degrees at work we got home and had dinner, then he insisted we drive to the lake to cool off. Being set in my ways to just relax and chill at home is what I wanted, not thinking of anyone else. I would gladly take off in a second when I was younger with my kids for tons of fun. I proceeded to feel a pout of anger coming on as I had no idea why. My emotions don't tell me at all, so I just get madder in moments like a child. Call me a kid if you may, but I was determined to stay at home, making my husband and daughter unhappy about the mood I chose to be in. I did go, of course and I cooled off at the so-called fun river, forcing myself to smile. Then after all the funny faces my husband does to get me to smile for real was not working so well. I got wet as soon as a few minutes later my husband jumps in. When I am mad at nothing but nonsense of my own being, I get madder. My husband came up to me in the shallow water where I stood and ask me what is wrong. With tender silence, he held me in his arms and the tears came. It was near the end of July and soon to be August that entered one year of my father's passing. I had a blast after that and felt so much better. That hit me hard and personally never saw that coming. I would, as a child, deliberately throw a tantrum because I wanted my candy or doll and go wild on the floor at the store to see if I could get what I want. In many cases, as a child, I would get what I deserved, which was punishment. The wonder still stands that when and if maturity in middle age ever comes to a level to stop and breathe I pray it ends all nonsense in me by all means. We have listened to our kids for years and now practicing to just listen to others patiently can drive me to wanting to put on earphones and pretend to hear. So patience and understanding with our babies that if anyone messed with that they would never want to see me again, that's for sure. So where do our feelings go of wanting to hear a whole story before we're butting in to have our say? We are adults in this world, not children or adolescents. We are mature people who can have a family and pay bills, followed by owning a car, driving to our jobs as a grown up, headed for retirement. Setting an example for our grandkids now is a scary thought when we embarrass our own children, while we take the time to care for grandchildren who, by the way, look up to us. So if we are acting like a nut, don't be too sure the grandkids won't pick up on it and tell on us. Hearing is a great sense when you can actually have no problem with it. My brain can't seem to connect with my ears these days. I ask to have the volume up on the television or radio when everyone else says it's too high. I should be able to enjoy entertainment with my family and loved ones just like they do, except with high volume that is allowing others to wear ear plugs. How disturbing you may think it is for them more than me because it's three against one or maybe more at a family gathering. Now, plugging in some earphones to my computer is great and the sound reeks loud enough for me along with my IPhone, too. I can hear it and I absolutely enjoy it so much, until I get tapped on the shoulder, getting disturbed to a point of being reminded I shut out the outer world, completely in my little world.

Chapter 8
Jealousy Verses Maturity

Insecurity is simply ridiculous at my age, even though I hold my breath when my husband sees a talented singing artist on television who, by the way, is a beautiful female dancing all over the stage in a size zero. Then he adds how great the entertainer is then blurts out the drop dead gorgeous part. I took action without a word.

I hopped in the shower getting out of my not feeling to sexy work clothes. After the shower, I managed to wrap a towel around my body to be sexy, but in fact most of me was showing because the towel was not a "just my size style I used to be able to wear." I daringly went straight into the living room feeling a sex appeal and my husband chased me back in the bedroom stripping his clothes off. He then took a look at my breasts and said, "Even though they are hanging down there they are still staring at me!" The rest is history on how to get your man after a ripe old age to walk away from a beautiful woman on T.V. I happened to jump in the shower the other night surprising my husband with no doubt in my mind there would be enough room. I stood behind him looking at his body covered in soap, then he attempted to turn around and pass me to get out of the shower giving me a turn. His response was "We both need to lose a little weight so it seems as we cannot be in the shower together without getting stuck while passing each other." I agreed, of course, as we laughed again when he mention that it was not that I need to lose weight, but just tone up. Funny thing is, I still want to lose forty pounds so I am supposed to feel more desirable, but there is a small problem with this, I'm still over fifty. I had my skinny days and now it's over, so what is the remedy for this? Proceed to do all the above and let the man's fantasies go wild for goodness sake for a great time that last seconds, because who says we don't? It's also a good idea to roll play with your husband during this times without a problem, looking and verbally expressing how a handsome and muscular man looks on TV or even in real life. It just might make your other half run to the shower too. It's our turn then to point out how sexy the nuts are hanging these days when the snake between them don't look up to us anymore but still works baby! Must we remember the animals of sexual desire in younger times when we jump in bed whenever getting the chance. The effort it takes now is such a chore! My goodness, getting the energy for sex and please forget the foreplay now to save one breath at a time for just wanting to get it over with. Guess it does come in time when our bodies are just not looking so good naked anymore or furthermore don't sound good naked either with flip flops then bounces in bed. Just my size and one size fits all is so much an understatement that I think they or whoever brings attention to the public, preferably me, need to have models for this so in the since to reality it shows not to have any common ground. I personally wear comfy clothes that are loose, not trying to fit into the jeans I have had for the last ten years.

I got a call for another job offer with more money a few days ago and the funny thing is, I was not looking at all. Surprised me that I went on the interview seeking better pay with more security. I'm happy about it taking out of my mind I can get up and be at work at seven in the morning till three p.m. I have worked part time for clients outside my home and caring for my daughter, so I'm home for her more. But now I have an opportunity after the hard work of getting my insurance back again, for higher opportunities. I'm not looking forward to more crazy stories to tell about interviews I have had in the past months. Got to get the energy on so time will tell if leaving my present client to move up in the world for better security with retirement for me my daughter and my husband. Here I go in a hurry to leave my present client so I could make it on time to my interview with a new job offer. I met with him, arriving a little past three. I waited in the nice air conditioned room, out of the ninety degree weather that fine day. Nervous and excited all at once, I saw him come in the doors just a few minutes past three. I did not show myself as being anxious because to me it was so normal to what I have been through with the past unpleasant work search history. He seemed normal interviewing me without the drama and gossip I usually hear. The man bought a new house in Washington, moving from California. I was glad. To see the perfect normal was a blessing and more than a dream. We got the interview started and all went well with smiles and laughter, finding the new client is just a wonderful sweet man in his late forties with epilepsy. His wife wanted to have a caregiver home with him while she worked at her new job she was transferred to here. Sure I am scared of what I don't know about his condition. I have had patients with this diagnosis, but never had to see it happen then do what I am trained to do for the patients comfort. Taking a nurse delegation class in a few months is a must for administering medications. I have been studying epilepsy up, down, left and right since the interview. This is a huge opportunity for growth at my age and I am so glad online classes are available now. I keep telling myself I can do this without being scared if something goes wrong or I mess up. I am actual wanting to have this by now and all of it with my experience, but I am not afraid to be scared of a new challenge. Come on, I am a few months from turning fifty-five and I have fears yet to conquer? I will calm my mind, even though it's my heart that worries me. I realized I care, so what am I afraid of?

Succeeding still in the golden ages indefinitely enlightening. Let me laugh for a minute then cry and find out I am still so very human, while growing up with life no matter the age. With the fact in place it may be my age I am afraid of to not be able to consistently do this job. Get over it! I tell myself silently to the younger person I used to be and remembering I was scared then too. The greatest part is the interview went wonderful and now I am looking forward to the start date, September second, after Memorial Day. The contract is in order, which shall be released by next week as I got a call from my new client letting me know everything was being processed.

My first day on the new job was more than perfect as I so patiently cared for him. With my educational knowledge I was afraid to use because maybe I forgot or was not good enough anymore taking away my fears of losing my motherly instincts because I'm older. When all of a sudden the seizure was happening and I never saw one before in all my years of nursing. It took over me like one of my children in deep trouble, as I stayed calm, helping him off his chair with grace, while grabbing a pillow to put under his head. Clearing the table and chairs sitting on the floor behind him with my hands on his back I continued staying calm. In three weeks on the job I have faced six to ten seizures a week, surprising myself each time. No matter where we were, seizures come without warning. I felt like I can do it, like saving lives made it so unbelievably rewarding. One day I was a bit overwhelmed after a normal routine of the morning assisting with dressing then making breakfast. My client and I had gone to physical therapy for arthritis in his back. We left therapy heading home and as we entered the front door the pain worsened when his knee's buckled under with such pain. I helped my client to the couch for comfort and a heating pad reducing pain. It did not seem to help, so I was asked to take him to ER. I did so to find out all they could do was give out stronger pain medication, which made my client extremely dizzy. Well, at that moment, I was surprised the release papers were in order. After being there for three hours we went back home to a much deeper problem. My client was so drugged from the ER visit it made it more difficult to keep him standing, so I tried to get him to sit down and stay in one place because he was about to fall. In a second, I cleared the hallways with no danger of stumbling. Then suddenly I saw him falling and just in time to make him safe without injury. My client decided to try to get up after I was requested to call ER again remembering we just returned and I wanted to not get my client up or move till the ambulance arrived. Getting up in a standing position, I repeated to my client help was on its way so my client decided to lay back down on the floor, making it look like he never got up. Off to the ER again with a loopy client, tired and drugged on pain killers. To end the long day, my client was admitted, but heard it would be a several hour wait. So he called his wife to come pick him up. It was all real as all happened while I am thinking how timeworn I am, coming home from work getting out of my car was so much effort, wishing my body did not hurt. How fast we react to emergencies at any age, including mine. Giving so much at the moment, finding out our longstanding body reacts after the fact. I could not help it because you either go crazy working at middle age with stress or humor, so I pick happiness every day. There were many hospital visits with my new client, as seizures came most every day, along with the in-laws nightmare. Things became much more challenging each day with my clients in-laws. With several phone calls of I told you so all day to anyone who would listen to messages left on the phone.

Being the most of always right at all times concerning my client letting no one at all get a word in. The messages left on the phone from them were a reminder of how important it is not to go overboard calling fifteen to thirty times a day, putting my client's wife down and anything else in their trail of conversation for his care. I must say, it is a comedy act plus for some reason, I realized that all my faults from being young and naive puts me into seeing how ridiculous it is to act this way. In-laws yelling at my clients spouse and letting her know what is best when she has taken care of him for years. It really becomes a conspiracy between the fights on the phone and being glad because the in-laws are no longer in town, like they were the first few weeks I started the job. That was horrid daytime nightmares I cannot help then and now to hold in busting out my opinion at the end of each day. I am not saying it's right or wrong, but I have to stay out of it and professionally walk away

when it's over my head. Soon
after six weeks on the job this all
became more nerve-wracking
with the calls from the in-laws.
Belittling messages left on their
phone daily became several by
the hour driving my client to more
seizures than ever, due to stress
on him. I kept it up to be there for
my client, but at the end of six
weeks the in-laws of my client
decided to threaten my job by
talking about bringing in a
registered nurse to monitor my
client. He was very independent
with his own thoughts, but with
everyone piling up on him and
me, I then had no choice but to
put a stop to it soon, so I did
without notice. I called it in to the
case management before and
after. The in-laws called my
number several times once I quit.
I hope chuckling a little at this is
in order because I cannot
imagine my grandparents going
through this in middle aged
finding work situation at the age
of in-laws be so impossible to
fight against. How old do you
have to be to just get over it?

This has got to be a new age of immaturity past seventy we need to look out for. My grandmother could have never gone through any of this nonsense because people back then had consideration for others. If it did happen to my grandparents, believe me the silent movie would be a prize to see! I personally will take some time off to think straight again and maybe go into some other way of making a living as my birthday of fifty-five approaches in a few weeks. I ask myself again, is it all worth it? I again go to interviews of possible new clients as I shout in my mind "Oh My God!" I reconsider the fact I may be looking for other ways of income besides healthcare. My education on seizures moving on a professional note paid off giving me the feeling of life saving instincts still buried deep inside thinking I lost it. That emotion is in any parent, no matter how we age past fifty or sixty, ninety and so on through generations. If there is a breath in us, it's for the people we love and that never changes, even if I felt like I was working for some entertainment club. I have talked about the comedy side of advanced senior years which in fact these very people are in there sixties and seventies, acting as if they are two years old. This is an action of trying to mature into the middle age in all the wrong ways.

Chapter 9
Forward Flashbacks

Out of work once more, just
before turning fifty-five, I'm
understanding a new stage in
letting go of the young mother or
father giving a million minutes a
second when raising our children.
Coming to a new emotional roller
coaster to just let go and become
that young man again or woman.
Remembering when it all
happened before the husband
and kids. How free we are to be
able to have it given back to us in
the middle age this time for
yourself to build, just you and no
one else. We feel important, then
we look in the mirror thinking
silver threads of hair or not, I'm in
on this part of my life with hair
color of course still on my mind. I
know what you are thinking about
hair color trying to look younger
while being picked for a job just
for me has to sound ridiculous. I
am not old and gray, just gray
and mature, still looking for work.
By the way, my clients think it's

my own color. Of course, that's where the hair dye comes in, yes it does. I choose not to show my saggy body. While wearing loose fitting clothes I stand in front of the television with ten pound weights, fifteen minutes a day to become skinnier. Not too fit because the hair color is what gives a younger healthier look. The ten pound weights give self-confidence because I am able to hold them up. I believe they work even though I still don't have the room to squeeze into a size looser. Being truthful, I am two to three times larger, for the fluffy look. I told my grandson, who is five, I have to get rid of my stomach. He said "Grandma you can't get rid of your tummy, where would your food go?" Well it makes perfect sense, so I had to tell him it will grow back in a smaller size so I will be okay. I do not believe in hypnosis, but I tried a weight loss video once and believe it or not I enjoyed it at the time. Being an hour long, I listened for fifteen minutes just to get an idea because well, I'm a snoop at all cost to lose weight. For two weeks I somehow felt full more than usual and I was attracted to more raw and healthy foods. It seems to just be a little here and there, but I must listen to the whole hour to get the full affect.

It's been weeks later and on the matter of weight loss hypnosis, I personally did not feel comfortable letting a stranger on video control what's left of my mind. Cell phones at my age are in the way of real conversation when friends get together for lunch, dinner, coffee to chit chat about life in general and then some. I took a visit to my mother's apartment not too long ago and I swear she is the texting queen of anyone and she's seventy-eight. My goodness, when we were younger, electronics not being inevitable yet made a pleasant conversation a lifesaving necessity that happened to be two or more people tossing ideas around, sharing our lives by words and sounds of sighs and smiles, with no disruptions from cell phones. Can you imagine my grandmother or her family back then having cell phones and such electronics to call their kids from the garden while she picked vegetables for supper? Not then, but now it's true. When our own parents are texting experts we certainty can't even get a word in. All I hear from my mom is her cell phone beeping and she has to instantly check the message, reading the whole thing that takes a while. I am not too happy at this point, so as I imagine myself throwing it out the window something stops me to remind myself not to do it in reality. Telephone cords were in style, at one time, with no way of throwing them out the window because the phone would stay attached to the wall hanging out the window dangling. No insurance to cover damage either for replacement. I start to think of the things mom says to me about the past times of not being there for her enough. I stop to wonder that, while I wait, looking patiently content, while underneath my anger rises for her to put the phone down and stop texting.

In the case of self-awareness toward our own beauty, it sure is a different kind of a feeling now then in high school. A few gray hairs or a zit on your face now are nothing, but conversations of what medication is causing that. How dare the same story in high school come up when you get up in morning with a spot on your face hoping to hide it under your bangs all day? I just did hand gestures waving with one free hand while the other was on my zit. I do remember one story from when I was fifteen riding my bike, which now would be impossible for me. The bike was new for my birthday that suddenly turned into a nightmare for any teen. I came around a corner riding with my friend and all I recall is being woke up in an ambulance asking me if I wanted to keep my front teeth! I was just waking up from being confused, so how can my teeth be gone? I'm too young. I was told an R.V came straight for me, hitting my bike, throwing me over the handle bars, onto the pavement, face first. I was in the hospital for two weeks, but within a week I got the courage to look in the mirror in my hospital room. Scare the crap out of me! I looked like a monster and never thought it would go away. My front teeth could not be saved, so after the recovery, the dentist had to put in partials. So yes, I have had a three top front teeth partial for forty-five years. My high school years were awful with teasing and loosing friends because I had to wait till I was eighteen to get permanent teeth. They're not the greatest, but a point well taken if I ever had a zit now it would be hard to hide missing teeth too if my partials fell out. That would never happen now, would it? My friends nowadays would be over keeping me company and not at all embarrassed about anything wrong with me. For things we can't control now in looks, believe me it's a permanent thing now and does not go away. We just handle it better and laugh when our grandkids point it out in a crowd so every stranger in the room can say how cute it is for what they just said. But picture this in high school, when someone in the cool crowd points you out and embarrassment never comes to an end for at least a week later. Feels so good to laugh at ourselves now in the present time verses in younger years except when my best friend points out in private I'm in need of another hair dye treatment. Now we should be thankful there's toilet paper, when everything in our lives seems to make you feel your age, you have some comfort. I have to just accept change and still be glad toilet paper has no permanent damage of change through the years because it will always reduplicate the same idea of use. Be nice if toilet paper was recognized as an achievement for us golden agers to make it this far in economy without change. That's what they mean when they say "The Little Things Count!" I am more than glad toilet paper is not out of style like most of the obvious all around us with electronics and phones. Let's not forget face lifts, with so many doctors there is a million ways to get one. Young years as a mother all I had time for was keeping dirty diapers changed and babies bathed, so where was the time for us to just sit for a moment wondering how to get a face lift when you told your children so many times if they pout for long periods of time their face got stuck like that. We do not want to scare our children by seeing us get permanent plastic surgery, so they see that pouting is no longer an option. Here we are with so much memory from when we were young of how different all things looked. When all feelings are put aside a new middle age of puberty grabs us as we are working full-time, learning to let go of that part-time working parent that seemed to have a family to raise, coming home to children, putting time aside for home work, dinner, followed by baths and bedtime stories. For the first time we are working fulltime without family responsibilities with small children. Learning to believe in us in a different age is alright now for the middle age working field which makes an amazing accomplishment. I feel like I just came to a point in my life enjoying the income for whatever my own choices are now. This was the hardest it has ever been for me never forgetting as I still struggle in reminiscences when my children were young. Through this, on a daily basis, I know it's all ok even now to let go, giving this opportunity to only me. Do not look back I say while marching forward to me in the happy dance. Did I just walk out of my mother's welcome party to her new apartment party? Wow, that was really a crowd in a two bedroom. The most attention-grabbing thought is all who came were people I knew years ago. Even ones I used to babysit for when I was a kid. Is this a middle age flashback? When I see other age groups coming in the door that my mother has been friends with for years I think in a different way now. Trying to be realistic that they are all mostly still alive. If asked I would never babysit their kids again, as brats they were back then. I hated waiting till two a.m. for them to come home from parties and I got twenty bucks, which was big back then, but now, no way. I can't stay awake past my bedtime of eight p.m.

Speaking of bed, I am writing again now being off work again. As I concentrate in the bedroom at my computer desk, my husband comes up behind me and kisses my right ear as he attempts to lift me out of my chair and throw me on the bed in one whooping drop! We were both half on the bed and the first thing I ask as we both were laughing was if he hurt himself. Of course he said yes, still laughing so hard we both just hung there in each other's arms, trying to figure out how to get back up. He said I had to get off him before he could get up. So I proceeded with my own strength to manage this as finally we were standing again. I had to mention with a smile that I was more than happy we did not have a roller bed, for then I may have further went as I was thrown on the bed. Now I know why we get called kids at our age from seniors in their late seventies and eighties, just don't dip me while dancing anymore. Am I the only one wearing diapers again after all these years? As I see my daughter dancing with only a diaper on, at thirty-three years old in the hallway one morning just about busted me out laughing with a leak or two if you know what I mean. Yes my kids are at the age where that good old protection is reality. But if I would ever think to wear diapers that fit me while raising my kids, I would have been able to go at any time without an audience at the bathroom door.

Chapter 10
Time Flies

There is a weekend I cannot forget, as fear set in like remembering waiting up for my kid's years ago when they were out with friends on a Saturday night. Now years later, its nine a.m. Sunday morning and all seemed so wonderful with my husband and myself when he decided to go on a fishing trip. We said our goodbyes, so my daughter and I soon had the house to ourselves. Enjoying the day until time flew by and already it was four in the late afternoon. I called his cell phone several times, but it only went to the answer machine. He was supposed to go to his sister's house by four, but I called her and he never showed. Seven p.m. to ten p.m. I got scared and called his sister again, making my daughter and all of us terrified. It was a long night of darkness with nothing to go by. Five thirty a.m. came at a slow pace when sleep was not even a thought, as I waited up till early hours of the morning. I called in to my new job, stating my husband was missing and the police were looking for him. You are never too old to worry, even though as we age, it's harder on our bodies, but we do it anyway. Finally, I get a call from him and I was excited to hear he was ok. You do not go on a fishing trip with your buddies leaving your cell phone on the deck by accident. Then deciding I know where you are by staying on the boat all night. Can you ground your husband after years of marriage? We must understand this so much more in our middle years with just as much frustrations. I need to go fishing by myself, very soon, I'm sure of it.

Stress of the matter of my husband's behavior came to a slow ease as we started remodeling on a rental we had. Fixing it up in hopes of selling the house we lived in finally on a positive road for once. Worries started to disappear in time, just like broken hearts and off to a new but more mature world of life, conquering yet another stage of middle age puberty.

I feel like I am starting from the beginning again as I go from one job interview to another. The first call I get after all this, is from a man in his forties in need of someone to make him breakfast in the mornings. The interview went good as he seemed to talk about interviewing thirteen caregivers before approaching me, still not being able to make up his mind. I was told he will call me by the end of the week to let me know his decision. No call came in. Of course, I get more calls from heavy smokers, who by the way, asked me to come in for an interview then five minutes later called me back, letting me know the client was her mother of ninety years old, with being a heavy smoker did not after all match my dream job. Other calls, however, I addressed by saying 'no' due to not feeling it would be affective for me to drive forty-five miles every morning for an hour to be a caregiver for such a short time each day. Then some possibly good news comes in as an old client calls me and wants me back. Delighted as I could be, I'm waiting for her to contact me in a few days, which turns to weeks and now nothing. I just do not have the energy to get mad anymore, for the reason that middle age is supposed to be set in our ways written in stone, right? I went on one more interview this week and I was on time. The person interviewing me was not ready for me at all. She says come back in a few days to do this again. What did I hear from her? Is it about my age? I became shrugged off? What to do when hair dye just don't cover the gray anymore. I waited till I got into the car to really lose it. I'm fifty-five now with my intention to work slowing down as I must to loose ten pounds plus I love food preparation with many recipes. My talents are becoming more important again while not

employed. I am overlooking my
goals ahead concerning
employment just wishing I could
focus on caring about finding
work, but in fact, thinking more on
my satisfaction of retirement
along with the benefits it brings
for all my time I cherish like going
fishing and writing books, with
several more to come involving
cooking. My birthday arrived with
such delight of turning fifty-five
meeting all my kids and my
mother at a special place for
lunch where my son works. Many
pictures and conversations later
which turned out to be a blast.
Come hell or high water I have
arrived at fifty-five. I am making it
through this mid-life ripeness with
lessons always to be learning
and waiting to reach the next
level. Fifty-five sure took me by
surprise more than the clerk at
the store when I got in line to pay
for one item. The clerk asked me
if I was fifty-five or older and I
became confused and thought I
may be being carded. I had no
liquor, I'm just here to pay for
brake fluid, not play twenty

questions, thinking what business is it of hers. Not realizing that every Tuesday, seniors get the ten percent discount, so the question came naturally. I just decided to mention I turned fifty-five in November when the clerk said so calmly that I got the senior discount of ten percent. I got excited and happily announced to the clerk it was my first senior moment of being noticed as a senior and can't wait to tell my family. This was amazing to me when I happen to glance at the clerk on my way out she responded with hum, well, have a good day. What contributes on the discounts for seniors? Maybe we paid for so long they want to give us our money back. Suddenly, without work and insurance coming to a termination soon, I felt pretty cool to be a part of an in-crowd for middle aged. This is the age when temptations start avoiding us, such as a gorgeous man or woman walking by when you're out and about wearing comfortable clothes. It seems I got a look once, but it was not sexual mind you, just a glance at how big my butt was. I decided to be positive for a moment to smile in feeling wonderful in my imaginary world that my butt is sexy. This is what I am talking about when I have to take my car through admissions every other year. I want to go and update myself to pass the test of being able to take on the temptations of life. If I had a sports car with tinted windows honking at good looking ladies or gents leaving the window down naturally would get some looks.

It's been a great summer, but the winter has come too soon and fishing season is here again with stocked lakes. I love this as I bundle up with three to four layers of clothing to go fishing very early in the morning on black Friday.

One of the most interesting, yet unfortunate, things happened while I tried peeling an orange. I dropped it in the water with two poles fishing. I and my husband were getting large branches to leer the orange back to shore. Too cold to swim as we fish by the shore in thirty degree weather. Continuing to get the orange back suddenly decided to see it go far out in the middle of the lake like the largest big ball of orange fish bait you ever saw. Catching fish is more fun than grabbing a loose branch reaching out to get a lost piece of fruit as my husband reminded me I brought two. Losing my mind, focus and sleep at fifty-five, I drove my husband in the dark early at five thirty a.m. this morning. I needed the car today for an appointment. I wear glasses, but where does the road go before dawn? It takes me three times longer driving three miles per hour with night blindness. Head light bottle glasses is what I need now, just like in the seventies! On my way to another interview tonight with no time to dye my hair pulling my somewhat gray and auburn colored mop back with a ponytail I headed out the door. Getting

there on time, wishing I was
twenty pounds lighter or younger,
I walked up to the front door of
the apartment building downtown.
The interview went well as I left
with head to toe happy thoughts,
feeling like no younger
generation is going to take me
down, and this is my baby! I got
too exited after leaving because
once I was five minutes from
home after driving twenty five
miles realizing I did not have my
purse on me when stopping at
the store for a grocery item.
Senior moment or what in this
case? Yes, it was. As I so
frantically called the apartment
complex to see if my purse was
there, the day manager was
about to leave by five p.m. so I
asked her to look around for my
purse. I embarrassingly called the
client that just interviewed me
and I was happy to know my
purse was there. I turned around
after I got home and drove twenty
five miles back downtown to
retrieve my purse from the night
manager after the doors were
locked. Remember when you're

driving at night it seems to be just
as hard to see as early morning.
In this case, in my defense, I do
believe when you're at that
certain age of the middle crazy
old lady driver going after her
purse that thankfully was found
safe, it's amazing how
wonderfully well you can see
without bottle glasses.

Chapter 11
Young At Heart

I cleaned my house yesterday using every muscle in my body that's left. I felt pain in places I thought still worked. I am paying for it twice because I took off with my husband the day after, to go Christmas shopping three different places, then to the grocery store. We had a cart full at every store we went to with the car filled with excitement for the holidays until I got home realizing this all has to be put away. First lesson is: get a day of rest, then try once more to go a second round of shop till you drop, but not two days in a row. This would have gone much faster if the stores with battery charged scooters with carts brought up the two miles per hour on those things to thirty miles city travel. Taking the bus with my daughter to the dentist today was a refresher course for me as I used to years ago with my small children. I got instructions from my daughter and depended on her for means of transportation routes and which bus to take going where we had to go. The feeling of being a child again when our own grown children are helping us get around even though I did not have the car this fine day. It was not stopped short to stay home, but depend on my daughter for our day of events. She takes the bus everywhere, therefore when I don't have the car for a day or so, I make appointments once I have the car. Today I opened my mind to a bigger world of travel and a new word for cabin fever; a bus ride. Seeing a young lady with a baby on the bus ride was heartwarming, making me go back in time, giving birth, holding my bundle of joy who is now showing me the ropes of bus routes. The world is coming to a better time for us, allowing ourselves to know it's time to lean on that small child once in diapers looking after our well-being. The residing hair line that goes from where there was hair on our heads to our chins then striking peach fuzz face. Let's not get too excited about the mustache ladies seem to find on their lip after the husbands so proudly shave theirs off on a daily basis when we start to hear them say "Please don't use my razor." This just means get your own lady's razor for personal care. It is a nice way of saying women have hair growing in unfamiliar places too. It don't make us feel better, for in fact, we do use our husbands razors time to time because electric gets it off faster just as the doorbell rings.

I got a big hug from my husband the other day and noticed his belly was sticking out pretty far. I unfortunately wanted to get a closer hug," but seemed impossible. I asked him if we needed to go get bigger pants for him. Absolutely not! He replied with high authority of assurance as he then mentioned "My belly is my personal memory storage container." Yes, right, I thought, a memory of what he ate and what's next on the menu. I never grasped how convincing my ripe old existence was today, until grocery shopping at a big warehouse. Walking past a sample table of cherry mixed cranberry juice I casually took a small paper cup in my hand. Never doing this as a teenager, I found myself suddenly speaking out louder than I realized. I started telling the sample lady it was the greatest juice I ever had, loving it so much. Mentioning this over and over at least ten times not noticing at first several people were crowding around me. One lady came up to me in the crowd saying if she had not heard me telling how good this product is she would not have noticed. Others came by the dozens, overwhelming the part-time lady at the sample table. I was being cheered on by people, asking if I could stand here for the day attracting more people. I left in the crowd meaning not to startle anybody, but in my defense I'm good at something and almost landed a job there. I am still trying to understand why some light switches are not in their proper place. Makes me wonder if home improvement workers have meetings about seniors needs. They must feel it is so much simpler for seniors to have lamps, like we need more light everywhere to see. My bathroom light is on the outside wall, while I continue to try reaching for it on the inside wall after many years. Putting so much effort focusing on light switches turning a small situation bigger while spending much frustration finding your eyeglasses on your head really is around the same aggravating time frame. Entering the front door, I'm walking across to the dining room to turn on a light. This is why lamp companies make so much money. Entering some of our homes, we see more plug-ins in the right spots, but light switches can be miles away. I myself preparing lunch just spent five minutes trying to figure out why the toaster did not open a can of tuna. I really did this until I burst into laughter with my daughter telling me the can opener works better. Then looking in the refrigerator finding the yogurt in a box of twenty four attempting to open it. Holding the door open with my elbow while reaching in to pull the box apart took longer than I thought. The refrigerator door hit my head slightly as I finally ripped the box with no intention of doing it right. Easily taking the box then setting it on the counter obviously, a much smaller of task. So age makes you do goofy stuff, plus no one has any idea what to call us in this century such as the elderly, older adults or seniors. Sounds better to say stage of life or lifestyle of maturity therefore call me by my name please. Whatever's going on is we have a delicate matter with the situation. Every person wants to live lengthier, but no one wants to be old. Therefore, it doesn't matter how old past fifty and set in our ways otherwise what generation you're in to remember to just call us by, "Respect your elders."

I got the most interesting call for a job yesterday when a lady on the phone told me she was looking for a caregiver. I told her I was interested in the job, then she asked me how old I was. I told her I was fifty-five years old then tried to set up an interview. Another question came from her, wondering how my health was. Responding to the question I continued by saying my health is good for my age. More enquiries kept going on questioning if I can lift heavy objects and do deep massage therapy. At this point, I felt I was being interrogated, hearing what sounded like a family member, but actually a caregiver raising her voice yelling, "Can you hear me?" "It's more than light housekeeping!" Telling me on speaker phone what I need to do for this person. I hung up, feeling like I was fighting with a teenager thinking to myself that's it, I'm done, so in reality everything up until now has been work and it has been worth it all.

The birth alone was all I could take in naturally, to the joy of holding my first grandson. The emotions in my soul that day, only I could feel, as the rewarding times raising my children were over in my mind, but not my heart. I will say that holding that special baby, my grandson made it clear for me, I did it and this is my wondrous reward from God. My grandson of five years old, comes running in my door on Christmas Eve with one thing on his mind. Headed towards the bedroom door then hops on the bed saying 'Grandma, lets jump"! We used to do this when he was two and three. Now, a few years later, it's hard for me to get rowdy with him not worrying about hurting myself. I am blessed however by this young child reminding me of my son who is grown with a family now. So instead of jumping, he senses I'm aging and silently leans against me by the couch giving me love without realizing how much adoration I feel at that very moment. Our grandchildren bring us such a joy.

At one time, I was tempted to make cookies. After greasing the cooking sheet, I left my grandson, three years old at that time, for one minute. Turning off his evening bath water, coming back I noticed right off he was greased up head to toe! He explained to me that it was lotion for his arms and shampoo for his head, telling me he needs a bath. The energy when our children were small this in fact would be fast and simple. Now all I can do is laugh, taking pictures with my IPhone, knowing I am going to have to work twice as hard to get through this evening, before my daughter comes to get him. We are then facing a few days to recuperate from being sore from using parts of us that don't work anymore. No worries, we will do it again, because holding that little hand is the biggest gift from God that makes becoming older an amazing miracle of how big our aging hearts still burst. The warm thoughts of my son at that age, now twenty-six and married, brings me to smile about a very creative story with duct tape. One day, his creativity pulled duct tape to its limitations for play car tracks. He never let his sisters near it. Going into the kitchen became impossible because believe me my son had more than one strip of duct tape crossing over tabletops and countertops. Crisscrossed all over the house in many directions, as the little matchbox cars slid down the tape made roads from my son's imagination. Funny now in remembrance as I picture the thought of not being able to enter a room without running into duct tape.

Maybe the scarecrow is no longer swaying over the garden where children used to run, getting hugs then kisses from grandparents long ago. Our babies giving us once busy lives, now leaving an emptiness, from time to time. We never had a care strolling down the walkway day or night. Drive-in movies, hiding friends in the trunk to get in free. Date night in the neighborhood, while children play and adults engaged in recreational playing cards. The ice cream man playing the same music day in and day out. Hearing it suddenly stop while children run with a nickel in their tiny hands, excitedly awaiting ice cream. Running home from the school bus to catch old television shows till dinner. Playing football in the yard till supper time with the neighborhood kids. Our mother's making sure there's breakfast made before school. Falling in love for over fifty years was a natural achievement. Holding photo albums, now filled with pictures, even though the worn out plastic cover protectors kept them safe. Listening to grandmas play church hymns on the tiny living room piano, while families gather around hearing what we feel at that time will not ever come to an end. Calling on a rotary dialed telephone, talking for hours with no concern about wasting minutes. Going to school in saddle shoes which was the only style of shoe back then. The milk man bringing deliveries to our door every week and picking up empty bottles to replace with filled ones. There were no cell phones for our parents to reach us, so instead the front door opened to call out our names. Go carts and tire swings were the entertainment for hours. So, you see, there is a humorous side of aging because the memories make you smile even to this day. All of us, now in the older generation, will forever be in the past written and living lives having the greatest hand in the authorship of what was.

From The Author

To my readers: I want you know how much it means to me helping you all smile with heart felt memories for all seniors of the joy it brought to me in writing this.

Author, Judy Deutchman